Franz
Beckenbauer's
Soccer Power

Techniques/Tactics/Training

Peterson's Guides / Princeton

Published by Peterson's Guides
228 Alexander Street
Princeton, New Jersey 08540

Designed by Philip Jaget
Manufactured in the United States of America

1 2 3 4 5 6 7 8 9 10

ISBN 0-87866-097-6

Picture Credits:

Bernd Elsner (4); Dieter Fricke Bild (2);
Franz Woelzenmueller (5); Fred Joch (11);
Horst Mueller (1); Max Muehlberger (7);
Sven Simon (1); VSW (8); Werek (3).

Drawings: Adolf Boehm

Translated and adapted by Harry J. Saunders

Contents

Introduction

I've been crazy about soccer since my early childhood. That is one of the reasons why I am very glad that the world's most attractive and popular game is constantly gaining new fans in the United States. In fact, soccer is by far the fastest growing team sport in this country today.

In addition I was able to ascertain since joining the Cosmos—and being part of their championship squad that won the professional soccer championship of the United States in 1977—that the playing ability, the quality of American soccer, has improved tremendously during the last few years. I have no qualms in saying that a team such as the Cosmos would have no difficulty holding its own in the strong West German national league. Furthermore, I am certain that within the next ten years, American soccer players, developed in the United States, will gain worldwide recognition.

What could be more gratifying to me, after my successes in Europe, to continue where Pelé—the greatest soccer star of all time—left off? What a tremendous challenge, what a magnificent opportunity for me to add my efforts to the growth and development of soccer in the United States.

I wrote this book for soccer fans of all ages—between 8 and 80 years old. I was trying to tell people about the willpower and effort required, the training needed, in order to become a good soccer player. I describe the functions of the stopper, the sweeper (or Libero), the midfield player and the wingers. I relate these tasks as I learned them from our coaches at my former club, Bayern-Munich, the team that won the West German national championship several times, as well as the European and World Cup championship. And these assignments were the same for our West German national team, which won the World Cup in 1974.

As a potential reader I visualized two groups of people when writing this book: First of all the youngsters, between the ages of eight and sixteen, who use every free minute to kick a soccer ball around on any available field, in the parks or on the streets. I am addressing myself to them in particular when I discuss various exercises and offer suggestions that are aimed at helping them improve their own skills without special coaching.

And secondly my book is written for all those fans who watch the matches and are interested in the finer points of the game. I especially picked out the rules I discuss because they are the most important. An understanding of them will enable the viewer to truly appreciate an attempt made and a decision rendered.

An individual's effort, energy and technical perfection alone does not guarantee success in soccer, nor, for that matter, does physical strength and stamina. The game requires teamwork, moving around on the playing field as a unit, with intelligence, a sense of humor and an ability to react in a split second.

Put all these elements together into a pot, stir them up properly, and you'll be able to offer the brand of soccer that represents a continuous special attraction to fans throughout the world.

Sincerely,
Franz Beckenbauer

March 1978

I. Technique and Conditioning
Dribbling

Hello, soccer friends. Nobody knows exactly how it all started. But with my experience, and a little added fantasy, I can visualize how it could have started.

One day, somewhere, a boy was walking along when he saw an inviting round stone, as large as a chestnut—perhaps it even was a chestnut—which he started to kick with his foot. He enjoyed that a great deal, and he continued kicking it around until another boy arrived on the scene and they started kicking the chestnut back and forth between them. And that was the very first soccer game.

It must have started with a dribble. In modern soccer dribbling has become a very important part of the game: Control

the ball until a teammate is free, beat your man and then pass the ball to a teammate in a better position than you are. Or proceed on your own, straight toward the goal to try and score. That's the way to do it.

And this is how you train for it:

1. Everyone plays with a ball of his own. It does not have to be a soccer ball; it could be a tennis, rubber or plastic ball. The important thing is that everyone has a ball. Everyone starts dribbling in any direction, watching out for the traffic, avoiding crashing into someone else, being alert, feinting, changing direction, changing speed, just enjoying a good soccer dribble.

2. Two players stand twenty yards apart. They keep their legs far apart to represent two goals. Two other players go against each other, dribbling and trying to score. After each score the players change with those who previously acted as goals.

3. Mark off a small playing field; with a couple of corner flag-type posts make two 5-yard goals. Two players are goalkeepers. Then choose sides, but play with only three men on one side and four on the other team. The three players are supposed to only dribble with the ball and try to score. The opponents—the other four players—are only allowed to touch the ball twice or three times in their effort to score. That's not very simple at the beginning and requires a great deal of practice. But then practice makes champions.

The Wall Pass

Look at the photograph above. This is how we do it: While I am moving on the attack, with the ball on my foot, my teammate Gerd Mueller (Germany's highest scoring forward of all time) watches both the opposition and his teammates from outside the penalty area. He may be closely marked (guarded), but suddenly he goes into action, running away from his opponent, changing directions several times, but moving toward me. At exactly the right moment I play the ball to him and continue my forward rush. Gerd just directs the ball—without dribbling—off his foot and into the open area into which I have run, giving me a scoring opportunity. Or sometimes he runs immediately into a free position after having directed the ball to me, and I, in turn, simply direct the ball into the open area, giving him an opportunity to score.

It is absolutely impossible for me to remember how many goals Gerd and I were able to score by employing the wall pass, which comes off the foot like a billiard ball comes off the cushion of the table. But we will never forget our many successes: The German national championships in 1969, 1972, 1973, 1974, the

German National Cup championship in 1966, 1967, 1969 and 1971, the European Cup winner's trophy in 1967, the Europa Cup for national champions in 1974, 1975 and 1976; and with our national all-star team we finished third place in the world championship which was played in Mexico in 1970, the European national team championship in 1972 and the world team championship at "our" Olympic Stadium in Munich in 1974. Proud achievements, and the wall pass always played an important role. We all try to perfect it and make it a vital weapon of our attacking game.

The first player with whom I executed the wall pass was my friend Helmut Haller (longtime forward of the German national team, who played most of his career for Juventus Torino in Italy). He and I shared a room during the world championship in England in 1966. We lost the final in overtime against England by the score of 4–2. I was only 20 years old at the time and scored as a midfielder four times in six matches. I scored the first goal after a wall pass with Helmut Haller; my second score was again after a wall pass with Uwe Seeler (another legendary German forward). Both scores came in a match against Switzerland which we won 5–0. Don't you agree that the results I achieved should convince you to practice the wall pass and try it?

The best way to learn the wall pass is to have two players play against one, using two small goals. There are also two goalkeepers. The two-player team tries all sorts of wall passes; the single opponent just dribbles whenever he has the ball. Some examples:

1. The attacker, who is closely marked, runs away from his man and moves toward his teammate. He receives the pass, redirects it into an open space and runs into an unguarded position. He immediately receives the ball back from his teammate. This move has rhythm: Pass-pass-pass, one-two-three.

2. The next exercise starts from the same positions. Again the forward, who has freed himself from the man guarding him, receives and promptly returns the ball. Pass-pass, one-two. But this time the first player continues forward with the ball, dribbles a few steps and shoots at the goal.

3. After the original pass is received by the attacker, he, instead of returning the ball, turns around with the ball and fools the defensive player, who expected a wall pass.

Scoring

This is a very special chapter. When soccer started many years ago, approximately 50 percent of the practice sessions were dedicated to trying to teach the art of kicking goals and the other 50 percent ·to a practice match involving two teams and two goals. And while some coaches may say that such exercises are old-fashioned and a waste of time, I am of the opinion that there was not much wrong with this method and that that kind of practice routine created a great deal of enthusiasm on the part of the players.

Without doubt there are many other exercises that have to be practiced intensely in order for a team to play well. That is the very reason why I sat down and wrote this book. Unfortunately, there are many people who can't see the forest because of the trees. In fact it is a simple matter. We want to play a better brand of soccer. That is why I suggest we look at a match played under game conditions and learn from our observations how and what we should train for.

Goals are the answer to it all. The team that scores one more goal than its opponent is the winner. That's the most important factor and that's why we always train to shoot and score from all possible angles.

1. All players—each with a ball—start off in the center circle of the field. One forward puts himself near the penalty area, and a goalkeeper is in the net. One player after another passes to the forward. From wherever the ball is received, he immediately shoots hard at the goal, trying to score.

2. The players start off from the center circle, one after the other, working their way to the penalty area with wall passes. When close enough: Aim, fire and try to score. (See the drawing at the bottom of page 20.)

3. The defense has a goalkeeper and three defensive players. The offense, consisting of three attackers, is sent into action by a midfield player. The aim here is to get the forwards to coordinate their scoring efforts, learning to score goals under game conditions. The goalkeeper and the defenders try to prevent goals. When the ball changes hands, it is immediately returned to the midfield player, who starts off the next attack. (See the drawing below.)

Heading the Ball

Soccer is not only played on the ground. This is an old adage that, if properly understood, can decide soccer games. I can certainly stress the point since Bayern-Munich won the European Cup Final against Leeds United of England in 1975 in Paris by the score of 2–0. The English used their two attack centers, Clarke and Jordan, who are experts at heading the ball and scoring with it, having the wingers bring the high ball into the center over and over again. But we had been well-coached and were prepared for

their method of attack; we were able to decide most duels in our favor. My Bayern-Munich teammates Rainer Zobel and Katze Schwarzenbach cleared most of the balls away from the danger zone; those they missed I was able to intercept or helped get safely into the hands of our goalkeeper Sepp Maier.

Practicing the headball is well worth while for all players, irrespective of whether their principal assignment is defense or offense. It takes hundreds of hours of intensive training to perfect our headers. But when you finally command the art of heading the ball as well as my former teammates from our national team, Uwe Seeler and Berti Vogts, and others, then you too will get a great deal of satisfaction and enjoyment out of this important phase of the game. I am sure of that.

Here's how you should be heading the ball: Watch the flight of the ball. Jump up straight from a moving position. "Stand still" in the air, using your body like a bow ready for action. At the right moment, hit the ball with your forehead. Keep your eyes open wide and your neck stiff. Move the ball with your head in the desired direction—away from your own goal, to a teammate, or into the opponent's goal.

Controlling the Ball

The ball is the most important part of our game. Everything centers around it. It rolls on the ground, flies through the air, and changes speed and direction, yet it has to be brought under control while you are running and marked by an opponent.

I really get upset when we fail to score because players are not secure in bringing the ball under control and can't move it advantageously. When you go to a game, watch how many chances are muffed because of these shortcomings. It will make it clear to you that you must practice often how to stop a ball, control it and move it. And practice will enable

you to apply what you've learned under match conditions.

These rules must be observed:

1. Meet the ball; don't stand still and wait for it.

2. Don't let the ball bounce several times; control it when it first touches the ground and move forward with it.

3. Prepare the ball for your intentions. When receiving the ball know whether you want to make a high or low pass, or shoot on goal, so that you can put the ball into a suitable position without losing time. Always make your moves with a purpose.

The action you can best take is determined by the direction from which the ball comes toward you and what you intend to do immediately after you have brought the ball under control. Ground balls are accepted and controlled with the inside or outside edge of your foot. Your opponent can be fooled by some clever body feints so that he doesn't recognize in advance where you want to move to or what your intention is. Drop-

ping balls are brought under control the moment they touch the ground by trapping the ball either with the sole of your shoe or with the inside or outside of your foot, or by using your lower thigh. Balls traveling level in the air should be stopped in the air, brought under control either with the head or the chest, or, if need be, with the upper thigh or even with the foot. As soon as the ball touches the ground, you immediately move forward, not allowing the ball to bounce.

All this can be tried out successfully in a practice match, using game conditions. Three attackers are being shadowed by three defensive players. The moves are initiated by a midfield player. The passes are constantly changed. Some passes are low, others just above the ground, others higher in the air. The attackers practice receiving the ball and moving it properly, attempting to finish off with a good goal-scoring shot. The defensive players, supported by their goalkeeper, defend and return the ball to the midfield player who initiates the next attacking move.

The Various Ways to Kick a Ball

The boy who started it all undoubtedly kicked the inviting pebble with the toe of his boot, just the same way all soccer players start off. However, good soccer players today use all parts of the foot: the inside and outside of their foot, the instep, the heel as well as the toe. That enables them to make the most surprising and effective kicks. They can send the ball flat, just off the ground or high in the air; they can strike it so that it curves to the right or left, or give it a return spin that brings the ball back to them, after it touches the ground, as if it were a boomerang.

All this can be learned. Those of you who practice regularly and try hard enough will soon get to know the secrets of good passing and exact shooting.

The way you approach the ball is all important. If your leg is planted next to the ball, you will get off a low shot. If you are further away with your leg on the ground, the ball will rise. If you hit the ball in the center with your foot, it will move straight ahead. If you hit it on the left of its center, then the ball will move to the right, and vice versa. It is important that you know where you want the ball to go. Then look at the ball, tighten the muscles of your shooting foot, lift your lower thigh, and hit the ball cleanly in the desired direction.

As you can see from my example in the picture above, taken during a match against Russia in August 1973, my right leg is firmly planted on the ground, near the ball, pointing at it and carrying the weight of my body. My left leg, about to execute the kick, is bent at the knee, and the foot is totally controlled. My eyes are on the ball so that I can hit it exactly as I choose.

Endurance

The picture you see at the top of the page was taken just prior to the overtime period of the European National Team Championship in Belgrade in 1977. We were totally exhausted but needed our energy reserves for another thirty min-

utes. And this after having had to play the host country, Yugoslavia, two days previously in the semifinals, another match that was only decided in overtime. In this final match we were tied with Czechoslovakia after 90 minutes. The last reserves of energy were needed if we were to bring our opponent to his knees. It was not to be. We were still tied after overtime and our team lost the subsequent penalty shootout.

Whenever the subject of staying power and endurance comes up, I immediately think about these two matches. You and I know that the normal soccer game lasts 90 minutes. But my team, during this competition, had to play two matches in three days, and each of these games lasted for 120 minutes—240 minutes of top soccer, 240 minutes of soccer at high speed with constant action. You need to muster every last ounce of your available energy if you want to be able to survive in circumstances like those. It takes a great deal of energy and willpower. You can gain these vital reserves—which a top soccer player must be able to call upon—by training hard.

You increase your ability—the ability of your heart and lungs—to endure through running. We run for twelve minutes, measure the distance we have covered in that time, repeat our performance as we feel stronger, increase our speed and lengthen the distance. And we find that after a while we have extra reserves available, reserves unknown to us previously, which allow us to run still faster and further. And I would recommend to you that you don't go running on a regular track; taking to the hills or woods is much more fun.

In order to improve and strengthen those muscles required for top performances at high speed, we practice with eight players. On a small field four act as corner posts; the other four split up into

two teams, two against two, constantly dribbling at high speed and making wall passes. After about two minutes the players become corner posts and the corner posts are the players. We constantly change, each group of players going at top speed about ten times. Even the "corner post players" can be used for wall passes. You will be exhausted, that I promise you, but there is no better training available. If you take this exercise seriously you will be able to operate at high speed over long periods of time.

You can't compare the endurance of a soccer player with that of a long-distance runner. Soccer has totally different and special demands on a participant. The situation for a soccer player changes constantly. He must be able to change in a moment from a run into a walk, to stop, turn, twist, jump, dribble, shoot or head a ball, charge an opponent, fall, roll over, get up again and so on, without pre-programming, always adapting. This can't be taught in individual practice sessions; this can only be understood and learned under match conditions. The only way to put all your skills together and become a better soccer player is to play in more soccer matches.

Speed

The defensive units in modern soccer are a hard nut for any offense to crack. Every defensive player fights his opponent for ball control and at the same time is ready to support his teammate. The attacker has very little time or room in which to make his offensive move. Those who want to succeed have to be sturdy on their legs, have excellent ball control and be explosive. Players who are slow in making their decisions—slow in recognizing an opportunity—can't succeed. The training for speed and explosiveness is becoming an increasingly important ingredient of any potential success. The one who is fastest gets the ball under control first, and he is the one who determines the next sequence of the game.

Look at our sketch:

1. The team runs onto the field, one player following the other, in one long line. When a whistle is blown, the last player in line sprints at top speed to the front of the column, leading it for a few seconds. Moments later another player sprints to the front.

2. Another exercise employs the same idea, only the players keep a couple of yards between them while running. And this time the last player, like a slalom skier, weaves in and out of the line of running players at top speed.

3. Another variation is to play tag, just as children do in the schoolyard. Run at top speed in order to catch the opponent within a pre-set area. There are various ways to modify this exercise. You can have just two players chasing each other, changing roles each time they establish contact; or you can use three players—the first one chases the second, while the third one catches his breath until he becomes a participant when number two has caught number one.

4. Playing "Cat and Mouse" is a great deal of fun. Take a ball, dribble for a few seconds in a narrow area, make a short pass to a teammate and, as soon as you get rid of the ball, spring into position, five, ten, fifteen, up to thirty yards away. And do all of this at top speed.

5. Divide your players into two groups of say five players each. No goals are required, just a ball. Use as much of the field as you like. You are only allowed to touch the ball twice before passing it to a teammate. Everyone constantly stays on the move, trying to get into an advantageous position, free from the opponent and ready to receive the ball. Never stand still, move constantly, and always use your head to outsmart the opponent.

Strength and Acceleration

People say you can't argue about taste. Everyone's taste varies. Some people like certain fashions, others don't. The same is applicable to soccer. Some people only like the way the Brazilians play. They like the soccer artistry, the total control of the ball, the tricks, the surprises. Again, others like to play soccer as if it were a game of chess, totally preprogrammed. They sit down and discuss systems and moves, which are initiated by the coaches and performed by the teams. However, the expert knows that these artistic abilities and these tactical maneuvers by themselves, or even if combined, do not suffice.

If you want to play good soccer you have to realize that it is a game that requires fighting spirit. The full utilization of all parts of the body is mandatory. We need to be able to use repeatedly all of our muscle power when we sprint, jump, shoot or head the ball. We must be prepared to make physical contact with opponents without fear of injury. And to strengthen our muscles we must exercise them.

1. Two players train one another. One player lies on the ground on his stomach. The other player throws the ball to him for a header. In a split second he explodes from the ground, heads the ball back to his partner, and almost on contact collapses back to the ground into the "belly" position. Do this about ten times, then change positions with your partner. This increases your speed and your ability to react promptly to a given game situation, and strengthens your muscles at the same time.

2. Use a medicine ball. They are nice and heavy and weigh something like ten pounds. See the photos below. I am lying down on my back, with my legs slightly spread out but fully extended. The ball is behind my head. I pick it up with outstretched arms, lift it over my head with both hands and bring the ball forward toward my knees. The legs don't touch the ground. Do this exercise about ten or twelve times and you will find that you add considerable strength to your stomach muscles.

3. Or you can use another method. Lie down on your stomach, fully stretched out, your legs slightly off the ground. With outstretched hands grab the medicine ball, lift it, and start swaying back and forth. Again, this is an excellent exercise to strengthen your muscles.

4. Carry your partner on your back, starting at the goal line and finishing at the center of the field. Then change positions—he carries you back to the goal. But don't walk; run as fast as you can. We call this game "Horse and Rider."

5. Play soccer as Horse and Rider, controlling the ball while carrying a player on your back.

Agility

Agility and conditioning are the cornerstones of a good, well-played soccer match. Only with them can you meet the tactical requirements of a game. Those who are not physically fit can't fulfill the given assignments either on attack or on defense. Therefore it is absolutely necessary that you work out daily with the ball, improve your strength, increase your speed and your endurance, as well as your agility.

In any good match you can watch how important agility is to a soccer player. When a goalkeeper suddenly flies through the air to make a save, then lands safely, that is agility. When a forward turns "on a dime," when a winger dribbles and feints his way through defenders, that is agility. And when a midfielder rises into the air to head a ball while being tackled by an opponent, or a strong and accurate volley is taken under match conditions in mid-air, that too is agility.

Good soccer players are agile. They are able to control both their bodies and the ball in all game conditions. Look at the photo on your left. It was taken during the very last minutes of the World Cup final between West Germany and Holland. We were leading by the score of 2–1 and our Dutch opponents were pressing to score the tying goal. It took a lot of strength and agility to get the ball out of the danger zone. You need guts to do that, and you have to train daily to be able to call on the required strength when needed.

1. Look at the exercise below. Use the railing surrounding the playing field if there is one. Jump over it, crawl underneath it, once the length of the field; do the whole exercise on the run.

2. All somersault exercises are helpful to increase your agility.

3. Juggle the ball in the air. Or play soccer tennis: Without allowing the ball to touch the ground, pass it between one another and lift it, with your head or feet, across a dividing net to your opponent who, in turn, also keeps it in the air. This is an excellent agility exercise, which at the same time is a great deal of fun.

II. Defensive Tactics
Second Effort

The idea of playing soccer, the principle of it, is a very simple one, known to everyone: Score goals and prevent the opposition from scoring goals. That's it, nothing more and nothing less. The team that has control of the ball attacks in order to score goals and win the match. The team on defense tries to stop the opponent from scoring goals in order not to lose the game. Whenever the other team gains possession of the ball, the tasks of the two teams change. Attack begins the moment you get possession of the ball; defense starts the moment you lose the ball.

The very first defensive weapon is second effort, a necessity I want to talk about now. While it is understandable that a forward wants a short rest after having lost the ball to a defensive player, from the tactical point of view such an "interlude" is inexcusable. There is just no way a forward can take a rest after losing the ball. His immediate reaction must be a total effort to go after the ball once again, to try to regain control from the opponent. There is just no such thing as giving up. Put pressure on your opponent immediately, go after him, force

him to make an inaccurate pass, or try and regain control of the ball yourself.

The series of pictures on the left explains what I mean. The opposing player, No. 9, has beaten me with the ball. I immediately turn on my heel and go after him. This way I can prevent him from making the next move the way he wants to. I force his pace.

We train for these second efforts, these attempts to regain control of the ball and the pace of the game. A goal is set up, and the goalkeeper is supported by four defensive players. The opponent's attack consists of three forwards supported by two midfield players. These midfield players, while backing up their own forwards, have the additional task of defending two small 9-foot goals, set up at midfield. Whenever the defensive players gain control of the ball, they immediately start attacking the two goals of the "attackers." This forces the forwards to become, at least temporarily, defenders. If they didn't insert themselves into the game as defenders, the other squad would be able to score at will because the two midfielders would be in no position to stop the onslaught on their own.

Dictating the Speed of the Game

People say that good players have eyes in the back of their heads. That of course is only an expression, a description of their talent, and we, who are in soccer, know what is meant by that phrase. Good players watch the game at all times. They know not only what is happening at the moment, but they anticipate the next offensive as well as defensive moves. In that way they are always prepared and never surprised.

As a defensive player I know when I have to attack an opponent immediately and when I can give the opponent some limited room in which to move. When we are close to our goal and other teammates back me up, there is nothing else to do but to immediately tackle the attacker, to prevent him from shooting and possibly scoring. If we are not successful immediately, one of my teammates will take over. Prevent the possibility of a shot and you can prevent a score.

The situation changes in midfield where the opposition may have more players near the ball than we have. In a situation of this sort, we are much more deliberate with our tackling. We don't just blindly attack; we try to slow the game down in order to give our own players an opportunity to close the space in front of our own goal to eliminate, as much as possible, the chances of a scoring shot. This is done by moving back and forth just a couple of feet in front of the attacking player who has the ball, trying to force him to move to the outside, away from the shortest line toward the goal. If you look at the picture on the left you will note that I am fully concentrating on the ball, watching for the slightest mistake by my opponent. If it occurs, I am better prepared to get immediate control of the ball.

The best way to practice for this type of situation is to have seven attackers play against six defenders, one a goalkeeper, as illustrated below. The game always starts in midfield. As quickly as possible four of the defenders get into the proper defensive position in their own extended goal area while the fifth defender slows down the ball carrier, allowing the defense to "collapse" properly. With a tight defensive group blocking off the direct line to the goal, it is very difficult for the attackers to succeed even though they may have two additional players.

Man-to-Man Coverage

For some forty years now the principle of a successful defensive game has been based on man-to-man coverage. Before a game starts, each player is properly briefed about the man he will be covering primarily and his anticipated moves. The closer your opponent gets toward your goal area, the closer you cover him. However, just to stay on top of your man, without adjusting when a dangerous situation occurs, may create even greater difficulties. From many years of experience in many international matches, I think certain guidelines ought to be observed:

1. If the ball is nearby, cover your opponent tightly. If the ball is further away, leave more room between the attacker and yourself.

2. Stay between your opponent and your own goal, thus obstructing his view of your goal.

3. Keep your eye on both your opponent and the ball.

4. Form a staggered defense so that the opponent can be attacked and your defender supported properly.

5. If necessary, and in given situations, exchange positions with your teammate when you can more quickly reach the ball and the opponent. Your teammate will then immediately have to take up your position and mark the player you have been assigned to watch.

The aim of man-to-man coverage is to get the ball when it is passed before your opponent does, by quickly stepping in between the pass and your opponent, or by tackling your opponent the moment he receives the ball. If you are unsuccessful either way, you will still find that a good defensive player is able to fool his opponent sufficiently to make him take the next move the way you, the defender, want him to. You must keep working on these maneuvers and make certain your opponent does not get the opportunity to shoot.

This is how we do it: In one part of the field, three attackers are repeatedly set up by one midfield player. Three defenders watch the three attackers. They are supported by their goalkeeper. The attackers are supposed to control the ball and try to score, while the defenders try to take over control of the ball and play it either to the midfield player or back to their own goaltender. The midfield player immediately initiates the next attack to keep the flow of the game going.

Zone Defense

The Brazilian team and other successful teams in the world build their defenses on "zone defense." It fits their outstanding talents, their experience and their interpretation of good soccer. They refuse to follow their opposing player all over the field; they decide instead to stay within a previously agreed upon playing area. Within that area they cover any opposing player. That tactic has its advantages: The distances a player has to cover are shorter; he gets less tired; the left- or rightfooted player can stick to his assigned territory; players weak in coverage can be supported better; and the general initiating position of a team changing over from defense to offense is superior.

In my opinion, however, not enough attention is given to the individual qualities and abilities of the various players when comparing and considering the advantages and disadvantages of zone defense versus man-to-man coverage.

Note the photo at left. One of my teammates manages to intercept the ball in front of me. Had he failed, I would have had a chance to intercept. If I had failed, there is another teammate just behind me. We are staggered in our defensive area, and that is a weapon of successful zone defense.

Now look at the drawing. Four attackers are sent into action by two midfield players. The attack comes from the left side. How does the defense react? Those defenders close to the ball cover their men closely; on the other side of the field, away from the ball, the area is protected with a staggered defense. The free player on the defense covers the side on which the ball is being played. On the other side of the field, the players fall back and draw together on defense in front of their own goal. This makes it possible, at least temporarily, to defend successfully against an opponent who is attacking with more players than there are defensive players. Of course, you try to have more players available than the opponent.

Do you understand what I am trying to get across? If I am asked whether we should play man-to-man defense or zone defense, I will always answer, "*Both*." I dream of Total Soccer: Defensive players insert themselves into the attack; attacking players take over defensive tasks whenever required. Everyone is constantly in motion. An attack over the wings is followed by another through the center. Close man-to-man coverage is accomplished by a staggered defense, with everyone moving, everyone constantly participating in all phases of the action, with and without the ball.

We should not play a single type of game with a single style. We must vary our styles constantly as the particular situation demands. A specialized player who can handle only one position is a hindrance to varying the game styles of his team. The more positions a player is able to play, the more ground he is able to cover, the more he can adjust, the more complete a soccer player he will become and the more he will be able to adapt to any given situation.

Attacking an Opponent With the Ball

In spite of second effort, controlled defense and a hopefully seamless combination of man-to-man defense interwoven with zone defense, the total defensive task is still not complete. You have to fight for control of the ball. Nothing is more important. The previously described methods only help to make our final task easier. A defensive player proves his ability by the manner in which he attacks an opponent who has control of the ball. In accordance with the rules of the game, your attack must concentrate on the ball and not on the legs of your opponent. To attack effectively re-

quires not only strength and physical stamina but also good eyesight and cleverness. One method is to slide tackle the opponent from the side as illustrated in this picture series. This sliding tackle defense was invented by the English. We should still be grateful to them for inventing the kind of soccer that now enjoys the greatest popularity worldwide. Timing is the most important element of the sliding tackle—using it at the right moment and at the right speed. Players accomplished in this defensive move, such as our own Cosmo, Carlos Alberto, are able to limit the effectiveness of the

While working out we try to tackle an opponent—sometimes one against one, sometimes one against two players. The most important thing is to capture the ball, to take over control of the ball, with the final objective, of course, to score goals. It all starts man-to-man. Those who are always ready to tackle their opponent are their teams' most valuable players. They determine the tempo of the game, they decide whether the team is going to spend the afternoon on defense or is going to attack. Their determination, perseverance and intelligence decide the game. And that is why you should pay major attention during practice to these man-to-man confrontations.

Those who believe they know it all, that they can't learn anything more because they are able to dribble or juggle with the ball, are dead wrong. They have another think coming. With that attitude, the possibility of improvement ceases. In fact, the know-it-alls' ability gets less and less. A soccer player never stops learning while he is an active player. If you have a chance, ask any of the great ones in this game. In addition, I know from personal experience that your ability to make any one specific move is only maintained if you repeatedly practice that move.

And even though I have made this observation as a personal one, great coaches will tell you the same thing, that repeated practice, particularly on man-to-man tackles, is of paramount importance and should be included without fail in every week's training schedule. This has nothing to do with the fact that the player may have lots of experience, may even be a world-class player, or may be older and ought to know better—everyone should take part at least once a week in these special training sessions. Each man takes his turn being the attacking player and someone else the man-to-man tackling defender, and as possession of the ball changes, the task of the two players in this exercise reverses.

most talented opponents.

Other possibilities are to block the ball with the sole or side of your shoe, or to tackle the opponent physically—shoulder against shoulder—with your arms straight down at your sides (otherwise it is an infraction of the rules). The prime objective is always to get control of the ball. The best defensive players I know are men who tempt their opponent into a mistake. They study their opponent, learn his strengths and weaknesses, and while seeming to fall for the opponent's trick, lead him into the trap, separating him from the ball. Before you can say "Jack Robinson" they are off and running with the ball, on the offensive themselves.

The Goalkeeper

You can't blame me for being particularly proud of the fact that my former team won the World Cup in 1974. It is the fulfillment of a dream that I suppose I have had, as any soccer player must, since I first started kicking a ball. And, as captain of that team, I was particularly proud of my teammates because it takes eleven players to win the greatest soccer trophy in the world, eleven players func-

tioning as a team. Everyone was an expert at his position, at his assigned task. You therefore might be interested in meeting them and learning why they were so good at what they did, even though most, if not all, of them may have their equal in other corners of the globe.

Our goalie was Sepp Maier, weighing 173 lbs. and 5'8" tall. He is a complete sportsman. While training intensively on a daily basis for his goalkeeper position, he also plays tennis for hours and hours, strengthening and sharpening his reflexes. You can't tire him or wear him down. I think he is the world's best goalkeeper. His split-second reactions and his jumping ability may be equalled, but I doubt they can be exceeded. Great courage is his trademark, and catching the ball, particularly in a crowd, is his greatest strength. He trains for that every single day of the year. In action his hands assume a curved position, his fingers fan out, and both arms are extended in the direction of the oncoming ball. The moment he touches the ball it is securely grabbed, surrounded by the hands and, almost simultaneously brought into the body. If he is slightly off balance, it doesn't matter. A good goalkeeper falls easily and rolls over easily, without ever losing control of the ball.

Look at this picture taken during a championship match. He grabs a high pass in mid-air; split seconds later he pulls the ball into his body, fully protecting it from the opponent. Total control of body and ball. That's what it takes.

There are other goalkeeping techniques that Sepp practices daily, but catching the ball is the most important

and most fundamental. His goalkeeper gloves, which he changes according to the demands of the weather, help him as well.

My suggestion for training with a goalkeeper is rather unusual, but I think effective. Four against four, and goals can only be scored with headers. The attackers kick the ball over the wings, lobbing the ball into the center for other attackers. The goalkeeper decides whether he is going to catch the ball; if not, he instructs his defenders to head the ball away. If the defenders—including the goalkeeper—get control of the ball, they immediately send the ball to an attacking midfield player to start the next play, which, once in a while, could be a lob toward the goal from the midfield area.

The goalkeeper is a specialist and therefore requires special training. This training includes jumping, falling, rolling, flying across the goal mouth, catching, punching the ball, foot defense, turning the ball around the goal post or over the goal. Special practice is required to improve the split second reactions of the goalkeeper. He needs it all, and not least of all strength and courage. Constant practice makes him successful and reliable.

The Fullback

Our man on the one side on Bayern-Munich was Berti Vogts, top left, and on the other side was Paul Breitner, bottom left. While Vogts is somewhat small in stature (5'6"), he has tremendous jumping ability, is full of fighting spirit and has fantastic willpower—he never gives his opponent a chance. Though always fair in his tackling, he shows no mercy either for his own or for his opponent's well-being. Breitner, on the other hand, is technically a more polished player, with great finesse, who covers large areas of the field and is always looking for scoring opportunities. Both of them, in fact, are always ready to turn their defensive tasks into offensive ones.

We have special drills in practice for fullbacks: The goalkeeper is in the net. The left fullback covers his outside right, the right fullback his outside left. A midfield player gets the ball to his winger. While one winger and the defending fullback battle face to face for control, the other fullback falls back into a staggered defensive position. Once control changes hands, the attack is tried from the other side.

Thus a fullback learns how to win face-to-face confrontations and how to support the other fullback. At the beginning, before anything else, the will must be there. Then, the more you train, the more you try, the sooner you will become cleverer, better able to read the intended play even before it is executed.

Safety first! First of all a fullback must defend his own goal; only later can he become an offensive player.

The Center Back (Stopper)

My good friend Hans-Georg Schwarzenbeck has had to face the strongest center forwards in the world and has stood the test. He was a tower of strength in many of Bayern-Munich's local and international battles, and much of our success, especially under strongly adverse conditions, was due to his strength and endurance. He is an outstanding example of diligence in soccer training. Many players are born with outstanding natural talent that has to be developed and nurtured. He is not one of those. He has had to work hard on all aspects of the game.

Perhaps it has been harder for him than anyone else I know, but because of his effort, his constant practice and hard work, and his desire for improvement, he has forged ahead of many rivals to become one of the outstanding defenders in the world.

I think that all young soccer players should especially note this point: Don't rely on your talent, and don't despair if your talent is less than that of some others playing with you. Talent alone is not sufficient. Nobody is born the complete soccer player; not Pelé and not Franz

Beckenbauer either. You buy success only with hard work. The price is high, but whatever is cheap is of little value.

The special drills for the center back (or stopper) require work on both defense and offense. Special attention must be given particularly to headballs. The wingers from the right and the left try to find the head of the center forward in the penalty area with good lobs.

In the penalty area the goal-hungry center forward is guarded by the center back. They fight for the ball. The center forward wants to score a ball with a header. The center back wants to clear the ball away from the danger zone. The goalkeeper is guarding the net. If the goalie can get the ball and catch it, the center back guards the net for him. The security of the defense does not depend on the ability of the individual defenders but relies on their working closely together, their fulfilling the defensive task as a unit. Each one is dependent on the others, each has a job to do, but each man is also always closely linked to the other players of the defensive squad. This is the only way a defense becomes a unit, an impenetrable block for the opponents.

The Sweeper (Libero)

That's me, at least before I joined the Cosmos. I was born on September 11, 1945. I am 5'11" tall and weigh 165 lbs. I liked my role as the free man of both the defense and the offense, and I played that role the way I interpreted it.

I can best describe the sweeper's assignments by putting them into five different categories:

1. To direct the defense and help your teammates do their job by calling instructions to them. As last man in front of your own goalkeeper, you have the opportunity to see the total field and are able to recognize soonest the opponents' plans as well as the development of their attack. I think that is why I could direct our defense and assist in thwarting the opposition's attempts to get to our goal.

2. To intercept lead passes that the positioned attacker has his back to.

3. To cover for teammates. If one of them is beaten by an opponent, you step in immediately. He, in turn, takes up your position.

4. To cover any opposition player who is free near your goal and not covered. Thus you can prevent his scoring and, at the same time your teammates can continue playing their assigned man.

5. When the sweeper has control of the ball, he immediately becomes an offensive player and participates in the attack. He should either try to make a good pass in order to create a scoring opportunity or, as I have done often, shot on the goal directly.

The job of the sweeper can best be learned in practices simulating game conditions. Three attackers are brought into motion against three defenders who are backed by a sweeper and a goalkeeper. (Those are typical match conditions.) This helps us get to know one another, to see how we function as a unit and to understand each other. We try this for long periods of time until there are no longer any misunderstandings between us. The result is that we can almost anticipate each other's moves, react in a predetermined manner and obtain the best results without wasted effort.

The sweeper directs the traffic. Above all, he must keep a clear head. All defenders must know clearly what has to be done. That is the responsibility of the sweeper, who is the Field General.

Midfield Players on Defense

Rainer Bonhof helped my German team win the World Cup, just as Terry Garbett had a similar assignment with us on our championship Cosmos team.

A midfield player has to be able to cover his man effectively, and at the same time he must be able to attack aggressively. A good midfield player is an all-around player who can play any position, feeling at home anywhere. In addition, he is a specialist in free kicks, penalty and corner kicks. His hard and accurate shots should be feared by op-

ponents. They should often come unexpectedly, and are either fast and straight like bullets or hit with so much force that the goalkeeper has great trouble getting the ball under control.

Midfield is a large area on the field, in fact the largest, and it must be taken proper advantage of for best results. It is the midfield where the defense prepares itself and the attack starts. The way a team plays in midfield, controls midfield, determines the class of a team. All the best teams throughout the world—certainly as far back as I can remember—had their great controlling strength in their midfield players. They were responsible for the success of their teams.

However, one should not make the mistake of copying the systems of other teams. The best way for any team to play is to adapt its style to the ability and strength of its players. That style has to fit like a glove or a tailored suit. Players are individuals, not machines, and they have a right to be respected as such. They must be inserted into a team in accordance with their ability, to take the very best advantage of their strengths. Look at the players we have on the Cosmos: They are all different players with different styles. Dimitrijevic is different from Chinaglia and Garbett is a different player again, just as I am. Each of us has his own playing personality.

It can't be said often enough. The same shoe does not fit everyone. That is why a coach has to decide what player best fits into a given situation. For that very reason I can't be considered an ad-vocate of totally set systems; in fact, I dislike them intensely and am all for adjusting the style of play to an opponent, to take advantage of his weaknesses, to blunt his strengths. Great soccer players come and go. Their style influences a team, and specific maneuvers work well as a result of it. But when they retire and are replaced, the game continues, as interestingly as ever, simply in a different, adjusted style.

As a drill for midfielders, put five men on each team (without goals). Each squad is supported additionally by one midfield player. The forwards, instead of receiving the ball and moving with it, constantly feed it to their midfield players in order to create game conditions, both on attack and on defense. The opponent constantly bothers the midfield player when he has the ball, trying to prevent him from initiating an attacking play. And the midfield player, when the opponent has the ball, has to fight to regain control of it.

III. Offensive Tactics
Avoiding Coverage

What does that mean? It means getting away from an area where everyone is covered by an opponent into an area where you can receive the ball without hindrance. It means to be able to get control of the ball without interference, which enables you to pass the ball cor-rectly without being pressed. This has to be done before your opponent gets back into position, that is, covering you. It means getting closer to your teammate who is controlling the ball, offering your-self to receive his pass, and opening up the game. Thus the playable areas do not become overcrowded, which would make continuing constructive play impossible.

The player getting into position—avoiding coverage—is the player who determines the direction and speed of the game. He has freedom of movement and is not concerned with controlling the ball, nor is he under direct physical attack from an opponent, since that's against the rules. His movement can be monitored, but it can't be obstructed. Once he gets away from his opponent, moving into a free area, that's the time for his teammate to pass him the ball quickly and accurately. As soon as the first player has passed the ball, he immediately positions himself in a free area, ready to receive the ball back, just as I am doing on the page opposite in an international match against Chile. You are not through when you have passed the ball; you immediately position yourself again, ready to receive the ball. Controlling the ball means you can better determine the outcome of the match.

Whenever one of our players has the ball, everyone else on the team must be ready to move into receiving as well as controlling positions on the field. It's not enough to make a good pass and then stand around watching others continue the play. You must ask yourself: From where and from whom could I receive the ball? Where and to whom do I play the ball once I've received it? Where do I move to after I've passed the ball? A good player knows these things in advance and makes his decisions accordingly.

Our drill for these maneuvers is conducted on a small field area, with two or three players on each side. We try to keep control of the ball, moving away from our opponent, ready to receive the ball, get it, pass it, and move again into position, always in the flow of every move.

Playing Without the Ball

That title may sound funny; in fact it may sound like a contradiction. You surely can't play soccer without a ball. That's obvious. But experts will tell you that the movement of players without the ball is a very important and valuable part of the game. We mentioned part of it in the previous chapter. Getting into position must be as much a part of a player as his daily bread and butter. A player standing around must feel, right from the beginning, like an outcast. Getting clear, taking an opponent away from the play, confusing him—that increases the enjoyment of soccer and leads to success.

In the scene depicted above, and taken from a World Cup game against Poland, I have just passed the ball, though tackled by two opponents. This means that one of my teammates is free. It means that we have an advantage over the opponent by sheer numbers, if only temporarily. (It also happens that we won the game by a score of 1–0 and thus became a finalist in the ensuing game in Munich against Holland.)

The average fan usually watches what is happening to the ball and in the immediate vicinity of it. He—or she—follows the ball, enjoys crisp and accurate passing between numerous well-positioned players. But the fan hardly ever recognizes or acknowledges the required effort to make such moves possible. When the ball passes from man to man, over the length of the field, it usually means that everyone participated, ran into position, offered himself—in turn confusing the opponent—anticipating the needs of the game, and thinking in advance. This requires willingness, ability, and a supreme effort to help teammates over long and tiring distances. Without teamwork this can't be done. All for one and one for all—that must be the motto of a successful soccer team.

Take a look at the drawing. The player controlling the ball receives significant help from two of his teammates. They move away from their men in opposite directions, as if ready to receive the ball. The defenders can't afford that and move along to cover them more closely. Before you know it, a fourth player runs through the center uncovered, ready to receive the ball without much difficulty. That's the way to play without the ball, unselfishly assisting your teammates by fooling the opponent into a wrong move and creating space with your actions.

Having four players play against two is an excellent exercise to learn how to get free, how to play without the ball and to teach the direct and exact passing game. Another way is to form a circle, with two players as defenders in the circle, while the other four players constantly move around, offering themselves and controlling the ball. Whenever an offensive player (one of the four) makes an inaccurate pass and a defender touches the ball, the offensive player must move into the circle and become a defender, while the defender who touched the ball becomes one of the four offensive men. Everyone should be moving constantly.

The one thing that drives me mad is to see people stand around when a throw-in is taken. A throw-in is an advantage because your team has control of the ball. And if you are going to maintain that advantage, players must move, offering themselves. Without doing that you can't succeed. You can practice that in a very simple manner. We call it "come and go." When we have the throw-in, one of the players moves toward the player throwing the ball. Obviously a defender will follow him. That creates an open area into which a teammate moves at once. This can start a chain reaction, but someone will be free, in position to get proper control of the ball. The player throwing the ball determines whom he throws—passes—the ball to; obviously he must throw to the player in the very best position.

Controlling the Ball

One of the most important factors of the game, if not the most important of all, is control of the ball. All that means, to put it simply, is to keep the ball within the ranks of your own team. In practical terms the picture above depicts my statement. Players of the same team congregate more players in a danger zone than the opponent. That means that one man at least will always be free—uncovered—and we can move the ball around within our own ranks if we so desire.

There are several reasons for ball control. All of them are tactical reasons:

In order to get our attack going, we move the ball from player to player, passing it accurately among our own ranks, calming down the flow of the game and at the same time forcing our opponents to come out from their own defensive po-

sitions; after all, they want the ball, the control.

If we want to confuse the defense, forcing them to move around, we move the ball around in a small circle in a narrow area on one side of the field, until our opponents try to reinforce their coverage by bringing in players from the opposite side of the field. That gives us the opportunity to move the ball over to the other side of the field where men are now available for a direct, less hampered attack on the opponents' goal.

If we are satisfied with the status of the game—if we have a good lead—we play secure. We pass the ball around from man to man, on any part of the field, making sure that we keep total control of the action.

We use this very same method in order

to settle down our own players who may, during the course of a game, appear to be unsettled and nervous. Ball control allows us to calm our team down, after which we again will be able to determine the speed and flow of the game.

You have to learn ball control. You can't maintain ball control standing still. Everyone has to move into open positions and uncovered areas. Only then can you move the ball around most effectively, almost as if lines of communication are drawn across the field, like a net. Moves made without the ball are the key to successful control of the ball. They start the engines, they initiate the successful attack, they enable us to have ball control. However you interpret the game of soccer, it is movement of players, with and without the ball, controlling it in their own ranks, that gives quality to the game.

Control is learned in practice by having three play against three without goals, in a limited area of the field. A fourth person is added who always plays with the team which has control of the ball, making it really four against three. Every successful pass is awarded a point; completing ten passes without the opponents touching the ball is considered a goal.

Try it and you will realize that looking around for the free man; thinking in advance about existing possibilities; accurate passing; making best use of the available space; and last, but not least, constant movement with and particularly without the ball, will determine the success of your team. This is an undeniable fact, but it isn't everything. You will also begin to realize that players in control of the ball don't get tired nearly as quickly as those who constantly have to chase after the ball. Controlling the ball and having the opponent chase you around until he is almost exhausted is fun. Chasing the ball makes you tired.

And the same thing is applicable under match conditions. Chasing someone takes energy. Those who are too lazy to move into proper position on the field, ready to receive the ball if required, will find that they have to pay a bitter price: first because they will become defenders instead of attackers, bound to be exhausted in the long run, and second because they will be on the short end of the score when the final tallies are counted.

The techniques of the ball control and secure passing can be worked on in practice by having five players play against two in a limited area. Most people call it circle play. It is fun to pass the ball—if possible—between legs to a teammate and have the two men in the center chase the ball around. However, should one of the two succeed in touching the ball, the player who attempted the last, inaccurate pass moves to the center and becomes a defender, replacing the man who intercepted his pass.

Changing Positions

Most teams in the world today play with a sweeper (Libero), which means playing with a reinforced defense. As I mentioned earlier, the free man on the defense, the sweeper, has to back up the defenders. That means that if the ball is on the right of the field, he too moves over to the right to cover for his teammates should the need arise, trying to block the way of the attackers to the goal.

On offense, since our opponent often uses this system, we must find a way to overcome this man-made barrier. What we do is to appear to attack on one side of the field, thus having the sweeper move over to that side. Then, quickly and unexpectedly, we move the ball over to the other side of the field where there appears to be less coverage, where there are more scoring opportunities. This has to be accomplished quickly, and if so, we will have greater manpower before the opponent can adjust to the new positioning, before their sweeper can return to the side from which the attack is now initiated.

Speed and changing of sides are important weapons of the attack against a reinforced defense. In order to be able to accomplish these changes successfully, we must plan for them during our training sessions every week. If players are younger, not fully developed physically, I would try these moves on a smaller field; for adult players we use the regulation field. Five attackers play against three defenders. First, in a small controlled area on one side of the field, defenders are drawn to that area. Then, after the opponent has been misled, off goes the accurate pass to the other side of the field, creating an immediate scoring opportunity. If a player gets off a bad pass he immediately is assigned a defensive position, replacing the player who has spent the longest time on defense. This way defensive players do not get overtired and can continue to put the attackers under pressure. That is important because, at all times, we must endeavor to keep up the tempo and the pressure of the game, creating match conditions. Only if these practice sessions are conducted in large part under match conditions do they have meaning, will they lead to success. Everything else is a total waste of time. There is no need for exercises totally unrelated to a soccer match. Good soccer training has a purpose.

The Lead Pass

In many matches as a sweeper I became, at least temporarily, part of the attack. The game was not quite developing the way we had planned. We had to create new situations, giving us more and better opportunities to score. This was the case against Chile during the World Cup. In the photograph here, one of my teammates takes up my sweeper position so that I can move into the offense. At this point all the players, and particularly the forwards, are moving. Open spaces are created, and I direct a pass into the open area, into which my own forward moves to continue on his way to the opponents' goal. This kind of maneuver creates greater speed in the game. The English call it a "killer pass" because it nullifies the defender and more often than not results in a score. Czechoslovakian players are a little more friendly in their description of this pass, which they have dubbed

the "alley pass" because it is the very shortest route to the goal (while at the same time it neutralizes several defenders at once).

We have to realize that these passes require total cooperation from the forwards, who have to be able to create this situation by spurting into an open area, ready to take control of a long pass. These situations are created by moving the ball across the field into open, controlled areas. By doing this we also spread the defenders across the field, creating the "alleys." It all has to function like clockwork: the sudden burst of speed of the attacker in a forward direction, the almost simultaneous long pass. If the attacker starts too early and the pass comes too late, then the attacker finds himself in an offside position. If, on the other hand, the pass is made too early and the attacker starts his spurt too late, the opponent will be able to intercept the ball.

Young teams often make such mistakes for the simple reason that they haven't played together long enough. Too often the ball is lost through misunderstandings. To be able to play together as a *team* means powerful control. Everyone knows everybody else, knows his intentions, recognizes his moves and is able to react almost automatically.

In order to achieve this "blind understanding," we have three attackers practice against two defenders. The attackers try their best to make long lead passes as soon as the opportunity arises. If a defender intercepts, he changes positions with a forward.

In another training method the attackers are only allowed to touch the ball twice while the defenders are permitted to dribble and in fact are supposed to.

Our final exercise includes two small goals that have to be attacked or defended respectively. Again, attackers are only permitted to touch the ball twice, while defenders, who are a man short, are permitted to dribble. We always relate our practice sessions to match conditions.

The Solo Run

You know, sometimes it helps if you look in a mirror and examine yourself. Frankly, I have not been exactly satisfied with the number of goals I was able to score as a sweeper. I should really have attacked more and consequently scored more. In fact, I always had that intention, but often your own actions are governed by circumstances you can't control, which force you to push your own good intentions aside.

In any case, enough of that. Let it be said here that every good soccer player should be able to make scoring threats on his own without the support of his teammates. This is particularly important when you are pressed on defense. You must have one or two players on your team who can take a long lead pass, who have a good chance at getting through the opponents' defense on their own and putting the ball in the net. The very possibility of that happening forces the opponent to be wary, to keep able men back on defense because there is the constant threat of a breakaway. It helps to reestablish the balance of the game. We can't afford to ignore this method of attack.

The coaches of youth teams would serve the game well if they encouraged talented individuals, in given situations, to take matters in their own hands. They should not stop a practice session with their whistles every time a player runs off with the ball on his own instead of passing it around. Don't destroy that player's confidence; strengthen his belief in his own ability. At the same time, all young players should understand that they are not playing for themselves but for the team, and that their individual forays are only to be undertaken as part of an overall plan for the success of the team as a whole.

We try solo runs during our practice matches. After a successful dribble down the field, we either pass the ball to a teammate who is in a better scoring position than we are, or we take a shot our-

selves. The scoring angle determines our final decision.

You know who was the greatest dribbler I ever saw? Manuel Garrincha of Brazil, who played with Pelé on the team that won the World Cup in 1958 in Stockholm, Sweden, when Pelé was only 17 years old. People say that Garrincha practiced dribbling almost daily, moving the ball at top speed around all sorts of man-made obstacles: At intervals across the field he placed stones, bottles, trees, chairs, hurdles. More than once he invited youthful admirers to participate in his training sessions by asking them to attempt to get the ball away from him. Very few ever succeeded. He always was full of self-confidence, displaying the same attitude in practice as he did in a match. More than any one single player he may have been responsible for Brazil's having won two World Cups—in Sweden in 1958 and in Chile in 1962.

Scoring Goals Is Vitally Important

I haven't scored as many goals as Pelé or some other great forwards, but some of the goals I scored were important ones. One of these was my goal in England in 1966, during the world soccer championships, scored against the great Russian goalkeeper Lew Jaschin. It was a goal scored from a considerable distance. On June 14, 1970, at León in Mexico, again during World Cup competitions, our German national team was trailing England by a score of 2–0. In the 68th minute my goal brought us within reach, virtually turning the game around. Our great forward on that German team, Uwe Seeler, headed in the equalizer in the 82nd minute. As soccer history has recorded, we won the match 3–2 in overtime.

For my former club, Bayern-Munich of Germany, I scored all sorts of goals in both championship and European Cup Competition: some of them as solo runs, others off wall passes with our high-scoring forward Gerd Mueller, and others through free kicks and shots from a distance through the defensive wall. I am not really the goal-scoring type, but I enjoy scoring just as much as any other soccer player. One of my goals is shown above. The picture was taken during a German championship match.

Scoring goals has become more and more difficult because of the tactics employed by clubs that tend to pay increasing attention to stronger and more effective defensive play. This requires us to have more intensive training for offensive moves. English statistics show that 40 percent of all goals are scored as a result of free kicks, penalty kicks and corner kicks. In European Cup games this percentage is even higher—about 60 percent. It is my opinion that these special kicks, which are a very important part of the game, do not receive enough attention in practice sessions. Because of their importance we must spend more time on training for their proper execution. Free kicks, penalty kicks, corner kicks, as well as the kickoff and the throw-in—all of them represent tremendous opportunities and should be taken advantage of. Our two drawings depict just two of these opportunities: The one on top shows a free kick execution; the one below, a corner kick. There are many more possibilities, and all of them have to be prepared for over and over again. If you try often and hard enough you will soon discover the various possibilities, which will undoubtedly lead to more goals. More goals mean more victories.

2

The Midfield Player on Offense

Having introduced some of my former teammates in Germany, I should mention both Wolfgang Overath (lower right) and Uli Hoeness (above). (They play the type of soccer displayed by Vito Dimitrijevic and Ramon Mifflin, the Peruvian formerly with the Cosmos.) Their talents and their strengths are totally different. Overath is a player who, with his moves, sets up situations that eventually result in goals. Hoeness is a finisher, a scorer. Obviously both of them make excellent passes that create scoring opportunities, and equally, each of them is an effective scorer once he's been set up by the other. Otherwise they would not be world-class players. But each has his strength—the one gives exact passes, and the other dashes through an opening in the defense with a long spring and scores. They complement one another, and my ex-teammates from Germany are in many ways responsible for the fact that we won the World Cup in 1974.

Midfield players are often responsible for the fortunes and misfortunes of the attack. I have seen it work both ways. What is right or wrong is determined by the defensive position of the opponent. If the other team, on defense, has all its men properly positioned, there is no sense in making long lead passes and moving the ball around quickly. Who enjoys running head first into a wall? That type of defense requires ball control in midfield, moving the ball from one side of the field to the other until the opponent comes out of his defense, creating holes and inviting the offense to make lead passes to the forwards.

A different situation exists when the opponent has attacked, lost control of the ball in our half of the field, and we must make the next move. That's when time is of the essence. The ball must quickly be moved forward with the least number of interruptions, bridging the midfield as fast as possible. Long lead passes are called for, hopefully followed by two of our players facing one opponent, making the defensive task difficult if not impossible. Then you can pass between the two of you or fake a pass and go off on your own straight toward the opponent's goal. You can take advan-

tage of the wall pass if the opportunity arises and thus leave two opponents standing still.

As in every move in soccer, you have to learn and then practice how to make midfield play productive. We have found it best to have five players go against five in practice. One additional player joins whichever team controls the ball as a midfield player. He determines the speed of the game, the tactics and the rhythm— sometimes making short passes, sometimes sending the ball into an empty space where it is to be picked up by an attacking forward, and sometimes changing totally the direction of play.

The Wingers

There are various modern methods of employing the wingers. In Germany we had Juergen Grabowski (above left) and Bernd Hoelzenbein (below left); on the Cosmos, Steve Hunt and Tony Field played these positions in the 1977 season.

Dribbling and speed are important parts of any successful winger's repertoire. Our wingers have two different assignments: One moved way back into the midfield, offering himself for a pass, trying to draw the flow of the game to his side and creating room for the winger on the other side; the other winger is always ready to receive a pass and go on the attack immediately.

Modern soccer coaches argue constantly about the importance of the wingers and how to employ them. Some of them insist you should have two wingers; others are satisfied with only one. There is also the possibility of playing without any true wingers. I respect all opinions but have formed a definite opinion myself: Whether you have wingers or not, if you want to score more goals than your opponent, you have to get past his defense, and oftentimes that requires going *around* the defense, over the wings. In other words, I support wingers because they can be a real practical aid.

We practice going around the defense and in general the proper employment of our wingers by attacking one goal constantly. We use the wall pass, dribbling, other passes high and low, and shots on goal. The winger receives the ball from a midfield player, plays the ball immediately back to him and dashes down the sideline to an open position. Behind the back of the defender he again receives the ball, starts his dribble toward the goal and passes the ball at the right moment to a teammate in good scoring position. We try this over and over again on both wings until we have covered all possibilities that may occur in a game. The more we try, the more likely we are to perfect these moves.

The Center Forward

My good friend Gerd Mueller, the most successful center forward in the world over the last ten years, was born on November 3, 1945. He is 5'9" tall and weighs 165 pounds. Whenever our team went on a trip, he and I used to share a hotel room. Because we were always together we came to understand each other extremely well. He has scored some of the most beautiful and crazy goals you can imagine. His short pivots and turns, almost on the spot, in either direction, drove defensive players crazy on many occasions.

His winning goal at the World Cup in 1974 in Munich was a typical Mueller goal. He works like crazy practicing goal-scoring from any position and from impossible angles. He isn't the type of player who enjoys regular practice drills; he takes part because it happens to be a requirement enforced by the coach. But if it comes to special practice for goal scoring, he does not object to coming an hour earlier or staying an hour later.

What he does is not particularly pretty or elegant, but it sure is successful, which means goals. He tries it all in practice: short passes, long passes, on his own, guarded by one or two opponents, on the ground, in the air, with his head, with either foot, dribbling, faking, shooting.

A successful center forward must have courage, or as they say, guts. He has to be prepared to take hard tackling from an opponent; in front of the goal the going is always rough, and the methods employed are not always gentle. Anyone who is fearful is not suited for this position. You have to be ready to meet the opponent at all times and under any given situation, without fear for your own body. Courage is one of the most important attributes of a successful soccer player, irrespective of what position he plays. Cowards don't win any duels for the ball, don't get control of the ball in the air—nor do they normally score goals.

IV. The Rules of Soccer

The Ball, the Number of Players and the Equipment

The basic rules of soccer are simple. It starts with the soccer field. Then you need a ball. Both teams should have the same number of players, and the equipment worn by them should not lead to unfair advantages or endanger any of the participants. The ball is round, 27″ to 28″ in circumference and weighs between 14 and 16 ounces.

A player's usual equipment consists of a jersey, shorts, stockings and soccer shoes. A goalkeeper has to wear a uniform of a different color so that he can be clearly distinguished by other players as well as the referee.

In addition there are bandages, shin guards, goalkeeper gloves and, if required, knee-protecting support bandages and a goalkeeper's hat. Trained soccer coaches will undoubtedly advise you about what equipment to buy, and where, if your school or club does not supply the required equipment.

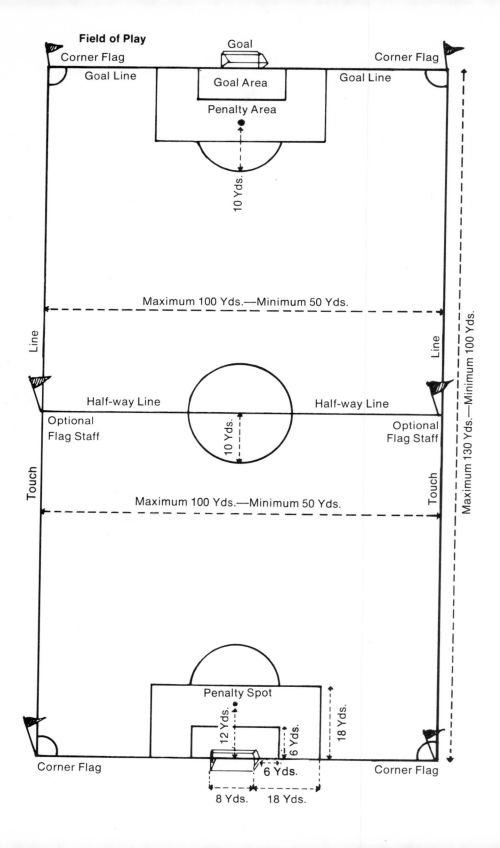

Field of Play

Goal

Corner Flag

Corner Flag

Goal Line

Goal Line

Goal Area

Penalty Area

10 Yds.

Maximum 100 Yds.—Minimum 50 Yds.

Line

Line

Half-way Line

Half-way Line

Optional Flag Staff

Optional Flag Staff

10 Yds.

Touch

Touch

Maximum 100 Yds.—Minimum 50 Yds.

Maximum 130 Yds.—Minimum 100 Yds.

Penalty Spot

12 Yds.

6 Yds.

18 Yds.

6 Yds.

Corner Flag

Corner Flag

8 Yds.

18 Yds.

The Playing Field

Soccer was played by ancient cultures. There were the Egyptians, the Persians, the Greeks and the Romans, as well as the Chinese in far-off Asia and the Incas in the Americas. History tells us that it was the Roman Legions who brought soccer to Britain. However, in 1350 soccer was banned in Britain because it prevented the youth of the country from "much more useful war games." But once it had started, its spread could not be stopped. The first unified rules were published at Uppingham, England in 1862; a year later the British Football Association was born. In 1904 came the formation of FIFA, the international governing body of soccer, in which all countries are united under one jurisdiction. FIFA restructured its rules in 1938. Today there are more than 140 member countries in this international soccer organization.

The diagram at the left shows you the required measurements of a soccer field. In international games the field is supposed to be no longer than 130 yards and no less than 100 yards, while the width is supposed to be no more than 100 yards and no less than 50 yards. The lines around the field are part of the playing area.

The Referee and the Linesmen

The job of the referee is to see that the rules of the game are adhered to and, in case of dispute, make the required decision. If a foul is committed against a player, but that player keeps control of the ball, the referee should not whistle the foul because that would unfairly give the defender a second chance. In other words, the referee should not give a team a punishment that is actually an advantage. His interpretations of and decisions about incidents occurring during the game are final.

The referee is the official timekeeper; he determines when the clock starts and stops. In case of a delay during the game, due to an accident or whatever, he allows for additional time. He is to banish any player from the game who has hit another player, has committed a deliberate foul or has acted in an unsportsmanlike manner toward the officials or other players. Without the permission of the referee, no one else but the players and the linesmen are permitted to enter the playing area.

The two linesmen (above) have to indicate to the referee when the ball has crossed the outer lines of the playing field and which team has the throw-in goal, kick or corner kick. Their prime task, obviously, is to assist the referee in his efforts to supervise the game in accordance with the rules.

The Length of the Game, the Start of the Game, the Ball In and Out of Play, When a Goal Is Official

Unless otherwise agreed upon, the game is played in two halves, each lasting forty-five minutes.

Prior to the start of the game, a coin is tossed to decide which team plays in which half of the field and which team has the kickoff. The team winning the toss has the option of deciding for the kickoff or the goal they will defend.

Kick-Off

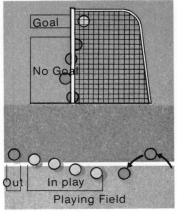

Playing Field

You can't score a goal directly from a kickoff; the ball must be touched by one other player. After a goal has been scored, the team scored upon will kick off from the center of the field. After halftime, the teams change ends, and the game is restarted in the center of the field with a kickoff by the team that did not have the starting kickoff.

The ball is out of play when the whole ball, either in the air or on the ground, crosses any of the lines surrounding the playing area, including the goal line. It is also out of play when the referee's whistle stops the game. At all other times, from start to finish, the ball is in play.

A goal is scored when the whole ball crosses the goal line between the two goal posts and underneath the cross bar.

Offside

A player is offside when, at the moment the ball is played, he is closer to the goal line of the opposition than to the ball, with the following exceptions: The player is in his own half of the field; at least two players of the opposing team are closer to the goal line than he is; the ball was last touched by an opponent; the ball reaches him directly from a goal kick, a corner kick, a throw in, or, which is unlikely, when the ball is dropped into play by the referee. (See below.)

In determining offside, the factor is where the ball is played from and not where it is received. Both players and officials have to be mindful of that.

Off Side

Unsportsmanlike Conduct and Fouls

A player who intentionally commits any of the following nine fouls is punished by the awarding of a direct free kick to the opposition or, if it happens in the penalty area, with a penalty kick:

1. Kicking an opponent, or attempting to kick an opponent.

2. Tripping an opponent or attempting to trip an opponent.

3. Jumping with both feet at an opponent.

4. Tackling an opponent in an unfair or dangerous manner.

5. Tackling an opponent from behind without that player blocking you.

(5a. You are allowed to tackle an opponent shoulder against shoulder for possession of the ball. The arm of the touching shoulder must be against your side.)

6. Hitting a player or intending to hit a player.

7. Holding an opponent.

8. Pushing an opponent.

9. Playing the ball with your hand (with the exception of the goalkeeper, who is permitted to handle the ball within the penalty area).

In addition, soccer rule 12 decides when the referee is to award an indirect free kick, to warn a player by showing him a yellow card, or to signal a player's ejection with a red card.

9. Deliberate Hand Ball

The Direct and the Indirect Free Kick
Direct free kicks are awarded for major violations.

Indirect free kicks are awarded for minor violations. A goal cannot be scored directly from an indirect free kick. Another player must touch the ball before it enters the goal. Indirect free kicks, made from the position of the ball at the time of infraction, are awarded the opponent if a player:

1. plays the ball a second time (before the ball is touched by another player) when kicking off, throwing in, or taking corner or goal kicks;
2. does not kick the ball forward on a penalty kick;
3. dissents by word or action from a referee's decision;
4. is guilty of dangerous play;
5. commits a dangerous play;
6. is offside;
7. interferes with the goalie when the latter has possession of the ball;
8. obstructs another player;
9. takes more than four steps with the ball in his possession (this rule refers

Indirect Free Kick

only to the goalkeeper);
10. persists in coaching from the sidelines.

When a direct free kick or an indirect free kick has been awarded by the referee, the opponents are only permitted to block the line of the shot if they are lined up at least 10 yards (9.5 meters) from the spot of the infraction. Only if the indirect free kick is awarded within the penalty area do different rules apply, as can be seen in the middle drawing. Opponents are then allowed to line up on the goal line.

The Penalty Kick

A penalty kick is a direct free kick from the penalty mark and is awarded for an infraction within the penalty area. All players, except the player taking the kick and the goalkeeper, must be outside of the penalty area but within the playing field and at least 10 yards away from the ball. The goalkeeper must be stationary, with both feet on the goal line. Only after the ball has been kicked is he allowed to move.

Penalty Kick

The Throw In, the Goal Kick and the Corner Kick

At the moment of the execution of the throw-in, when the player is throwing the ball into play after it has wholly crossed the touchline, he must face the field and have both feet either on the touchline or outside the touchline. With both feet touching the ground, the player throws the ball in with both hands from behind his back, over his head.

Throw in

A goal kick is made by a defending player when the attacking team is the last to touch the ball before it crosses the line of the goal they are attacking. It is repeated if it does not clear the penalty area. All players other than the one making the goal kick must be outside of the penalty area when a goal kick is being taken. A goal cannot be scored directly from a goal kick.

Goal Kick

Corner Kick

A corner kick is made when the defending team puts the ball over its own goal line and the attacking team kicks the ball into play from the quarter circle designated at the nearest corner flag. The defending players are not permitted any closer to the ball than 10 yards (9.5 meters). The player taking the corner kick may not touch the ball a second time after the initial contact before it has been touched by another player.

Soccer Language

Championship—A competition between a number of teams from different localities. They usually play one or more matches against one another to determine the very best among them. The winner is crowned the champion for one season.

Club Teams—A selected group of players, at least 11, representing an organization and wearing its chosen colors throughout a season.

CONCACAF—Confederation of North and Central American and Caribbean Association Football. The organization responsible for international soccer promotions in North and Central America as well as the Caribbean area.

Corner—The designated term for a corner kick.

Counterattack—A quick turnaround from a defensive position to an offensive one.

Cup Matches—A term created by the English Football Association for a competition in which, through the process of elimination, the number of teams competing is eventually reduced to two finalists who in their game determine the cup winner. Cup competitions are usually run in addition to regular championship games and, in most countries, involve both professional and amateur teams playing against each other.

Dewar's Cup—The United States Open Challenge Cup trophy, the highest soccer trophy awarded on an annual basis by the USSF. Competition is open to participation by all soccer teams across the country.

Extra time—The referee is supposed to allow for extra time if there have been unwarranted interruptions, such as serious injuries, during the game.

FIFA—The Fédération Internationale de Football Association, which has its seat in Zurich, Switzerland, governs all soccer. All associations of all countries throughout the world are members. It has a larger membership than the United Nations. It decides through its various committees when international matches are to be held, who is to referee games, and what the rules of the soccer competition are. All countries, when playing across their own national borders, ask for and obtain approval from this body. All countries have accepted that the decisions rendered by FIFA are to be considered binding and final.

FIFA Cup—This is the new trophy donated by the world soccer association, to assure continuity of the world soccer championship for national teams. The world championship is played off every four years. Regions determine finalists,

and the best 16 teams play off for the coveted trophy in a pre-selected host country. In 1982 the matches will be played in Spain.

FIFA World Youth Cup—This is a new competition made possible through the cooperation and financial assistance of a United States soft drink manufacturer. It will involve on a worldwide basis teams from different qualifying nations, made up of players under 19 years of age, only a stepping-stone away from top-flight soccer.

Foul—An infraction of the rules of the game.

Goalgetter—A consistent scorer.

Halftime—The intermission between the two equal halves of the game. It is supposed to last only five minutes, unless the referee permits an extension.

International—A match between two national teams representing different countries.

James P. McGuire Trophy—Emblematic of the United States Junior Challenge Cup Competition, this trophy is awarded though the process of cup competition to the best United States Junior team (age 16 through 18).

Jules Rimet Cup—Named after the first president of FIFA, the Rimet Cup was given permanently to Brazil after that country won the world soccer championship for national teams the third time. Pelé was on all three teams.

Keeping time—Keeping time is strictly the responsibility of the referee, who keeps a timepiece on his person. He may consult with his linesmen but not a stadium clock.

Libero—The Italian name, used worldwide, for the free man on the defense. In Britain and North America, the term "Sweeper" is used for this player.

Marking—To play close to an opponent in order to prevent him from receiving the ball or initiating and dictating the tempo of the game.

NASL—The North American Soccer League, the professional soccer league covering the United States and Canada, coast to coast.

National Coaching School—One of the coaching schools run across the United States under the jurisdiction of the USSF for adults who want to become qualified and licensed soccer coaches.

National Referee School—One of the many referee schools under the jurisdiction of the USSF, which are run in different areas for adults who want to become officials. The most experienced referees are advanced to the professional leagues and eventually receive the designation of "FIFA Referee" which means that they will be appointed to officiate international matches.

National Teams—A group of all-star players selected for their ability to represent their country in international competition. All players must be citizens of the country that they represent. Here in the United States, in other words, all players on national teams must have U.S. citizenship. No player who has played for one country in international competition can appear for another country at a later date, even though he may have changed his citizenship.

Officials—The only people directly connected with the conduct of the game, aside from the active players, are the officials. They are the referee and his two assistants, the linesmen.

Offside trap—A method by which defensive players move jointly forward in order to place an attacking player into the offside position.

Olympic Teams—These teams are made up of the very best amateur players of countries who try to advance, through elimination rounds, to the Olympic Games, which are held every four years in a different host country. The next Olympic Games will be held in 1980 in Moscow.

Overtime—Cup games are usually extended by two periods of 15 minutes overtime if the score between the two opponents is tied after the regulation time of 90 minutes.

Penalty kicking—The rules of a game or competition may, by prior agreement, determine that if a game is tied in regulation time, or after overtime, such a game is to be decided by penalty kicks.

Posts—The goal posts and the cross bar can be square, rectangular or round, and may be constructed of either wood or metal. They should be at least ten centimeters and not more than twelve centimeters in width and depth.

Qualification—An elimination match to advance in a cup competition.

Reserve bench—Next to the field of play, at least 25 yards from the outline of the field, is a players' bench on which five substitute players may wait. In addition, the coach and the trainer and, if desired, a team doctor, sit on the bench. In national competition the respective associations decide how many of the 11 starting players may be substituted for. In international competition FIFA has decided that only two players may be substituted for in any match. No resubstitution is permitted. These rules are often modified in youth leagues.

Rules—Soccer rules are determined by an international board, appointed by FIFA and made up of rules experts from different countries. They are responsible for any adjustment and changes in soccer rules.

Same level—If an attacker, at the moment the ball is passed, is on a direct line with a defender—on the same level—he is considered offside.

Send off—A player who has conducted himself in an unsportsmanlike manner, by committing dangerous and deliberate fouls, or by verbally insulting the officials and/or other players, can be sent off the field by the referee either with or without a prior warning. The referee simply has to show the player the red card. There is no appeal from the referee's decision.

Shootout—Strictly a rule applicable only to tied games in the NASL after regulation time and overtime which presents a series of one-on-one goal scoring situations (five in all).

Sliding tackle—A tactic in which a player slides on the ground into the ball, in order to take the ball away from an opponent.

Soccer Regions—Because the United States is such a vast country, soccer administration here has been split into four geographical regions: Region I, Eastern USA; Region II, Midwestern USA; Region III, Southern USA; and Region IV, Western USA.

Standings—The way teams finish a championship; in the NASL, their position in a table that lists the points gained, games won and lost, and the goals scored and allowed. Those with the most points head the standings.

State Associations—These associations govern soccer in every state of the United States. They are supposed to administrate national and local programs within their state and help to promote the game of soccer on all levels except the professional one.

System—The way a team operates on the field with its players, i.e. 4-3-3 or 4-2-4 or 4-4-2, all designating defensive, midfield and offensive player positions.

UEFA—The French-language acronym for the United European Soccer Federations. Their task is to organize and promote European championships for national amateur, professional and youth teams, and conduct annual championship tournaments for national champions, national cup champions and similar activities, conducted within the European soccer community.

U.S. Amateur Cup—An annual cup competition open only to amateur teams across the United States.

USSF—The United States Soccer Federation, which controls and promotes soccer across the United States. Its seat is in New York.

USYSA—The United States Youth Soccer Association, which controls, in cooperation with the USSF, youth soccer in the United States, starting with youngsters from 6 years of age—boys and girls—up to the "under 19's," all of whom play on local teams and compete for championships in different age categories.

Warning—Players who constantly infringe upon the rules of the game, or make disrespectful remarks or gestures toward the referee, or otherwise conduct themselves in an unsportsmanlike manner, may be warned by the referee, who shows them a yellow card.

MA'

S